SandCastle™
Mini Animal Marvels

Miniature
Birds

A Division of ABDO

ABDO
Publishing Company

Alex Kuskowski   Consulting Editor, Diane Craig, M.A./Reading Specialist

visit us at www.abdopublishing.com

Published by ABDO Publishing Company, a division of ABDO, P.O. Box 398166, Minneapolis, Minnesota 55439. Copyright © 2014 by Abdo Consulting Group, Inc. International copyrights reserved in all countries. No part of this book may be reproduced in any form without written permission from the publisher. SandCastle™ is a trademark and logo of ABDO Publishing Company.

Printed in the United States of America, North Mankato, Minnesota
102013
012014

 PRINTED ON RECYCLED PAPER

Editor: Liz Salzmann
Content Developer: Alex Kuskowski
Cover and Interior Design and Production: Mighty Media, Inc.
Photo Credits: Len Worthington, Paul Jones, Shutterstock

Library of Congress Cataloging-in-Publication Data

Kuskowski, Alex.
  Miniature birds / Alex Kuskowski.
     pages cm. -- (Mini animal marvels)
  ISBN 978-1-62403-064-2
1. Birds--Juvenile literature. 2. Birds--Size--Juvenile literature. I. Title.
  QL676.2.K87 2014
  598--dc23
                          2013022895

SandCastle™ Level: Transitional

SandCastle™ books are created by a team of professional educators, reading specialists, and content developers around five essential components—phonemic awareness, phonics, vocabulary, text comprehension, and fluency—to assist young readers as they develop reading skills and strategies and increase their general knowledge. All books are written, reviewed, and leveled for guided reading, early reading intervention, and Accelerated Reader® programs for use in shared, guided, and independent reading and writing activities to support a balanced approach to literacy instruction. The SandCastle™ series has four levels that correspond to early literacy development. The levels are provided to help teachers and parents select appropriate books for young readers.

Emerging Readers   Beginning Readers   Transitional Readers   Fluent Readers
  (no flags)   (1 flag)   (2 flags)   (3 flags)

Table of Contents

Miniature Birds

Miniature birds are small birds that fly. They live all over the world!

Red-shouldered Macaw

South America

The red-shouldered macaw is the smallest macaw. It lives in South America.

6 feet
(1.8 m)

It is 12 inches
(30.5 cm) long.

12 inches
(30.5 cm)

Red-shouldered macaws clean themselves. Sometimes they clean each other!

Parrotlet

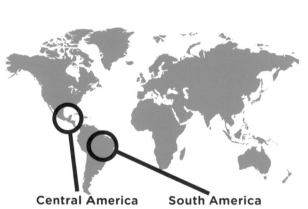

Central America   South America

Parrotlets are very small parrots. Parrotlet means "little parrot."

6 feet
(1.8 m)

It is 6 inches
(15.2 cm) long.

6 inches
(15.2 cm)

Parrotlets travel in big groups.
Parrotlets **mate** for life.

Parrotlets live in the **rain forest**.
They eat plants.

Bee Hummingbird

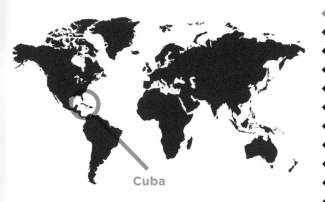

Cuba

The bee hummingbird is the smallest bird. It lives in the forests of Cuba.

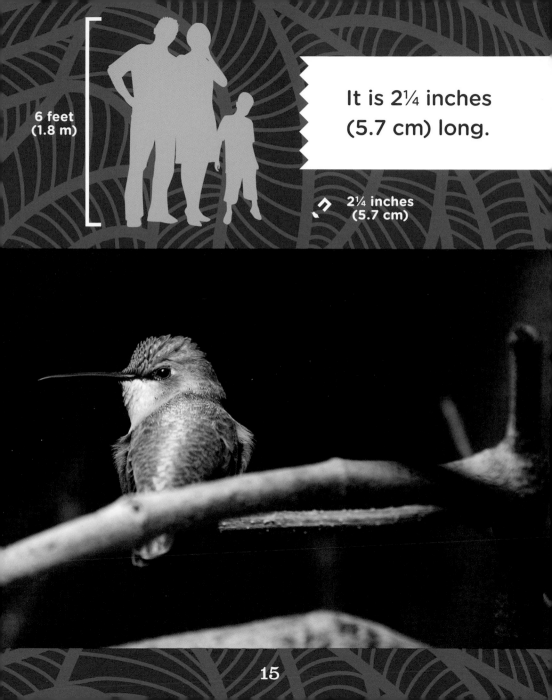

6 feet
(1.8 m)

It is 2¼ inches
(5.7 cm) long.

2¼ inches
(5.7 cm)

Bee hummingbirds have long beaks. They use them to eat flower nectar.

Bee hummingbirds are fast.
Their wings move 80 times a second.

Green Aracari

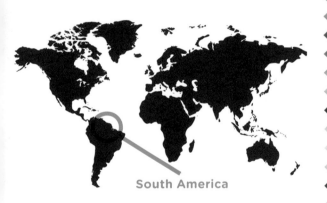

South America

The green aracari is a small **toucan**. It lives in South America. It eats fruit in the **rain forest**.

6 feet
(1.8 m)

It is 12 inches
(30.5 cm) long.

12 inches
(30.5 cm)

Female green aracaris
have brown heads.
Males have black heads.

Did You Know?

 Red-shouldered macaws can learn to talk.

 Some people keep parrotlets as pets.

 Bee hummingbirds are 10 times smaller than the largest hummingbird.

 Green aracaris live in holes in tree **trunks**.

Bird Quiz

1 Red-shouldered macaws never clean themselves.

2 Parrotlets **mate** for life.

3 Bee hummingbird's wings move 80 times per second.

4 The green aracari is a kind of **toucan**.

5 **Female** green aracaris have green heads.

Answers: 1. False 2. True 3. True 4. True 5. False

Glossary

female – being of the sex that can produce eggs or give birth. Mothers are female.

male – being of the sex that can father offspring. Fathers are male.

mate – to live together and have babies.

rain forest – a tropical wooded area that gets a lot of rain and has very tall trees.

toucan – a colorful bird with a very large beak.

trunk – the thick, main stem of a tree.